CONTENTS

Welcome	
Morning	
Wet day	7
Slow walk	8
I know	9
There is a loss, too	10
Language is action	11
To live time	12
Convenience	13
Climate crisis	14
Enamel	15
When the tents burn	16
Field to for –	17
What is your name?	18
River	19
Wind	20
Wren	21
Curlew	22
Turtle dove	23
Blackbird	24
Wake the night	25
Wild	26
Flow	27
Thaw	28
Heaven on Earth	29
Wonder	30
Clarity	31
Good things come to those who wa –	32
You can	33
Ground perspective	34
Beginning	35
Ending thoughts	37
About the album and author	38

WELCOME

You are warmly invited to dip, delve, or disappear into this collection. The poems, drawings and music have come to being over the past couple of years, centring on the idea of 'wildness' – of the landscape we inhabit, yet also a neural 'landscape' where 'wildness' is synonymous with creative wiring. I wish to re-wild the language around neurodiversity, harnessing its rawness and colour to express the beauty and fragility of our nature-home.

The project also focuses on the impact that nature-language acquisition has on our knowledge and care for natural habitats, with a section comprising poems 'naming nature' from a perspective of curiosity – yet also lament – for the abundance of the wild at our feet that we so often cannot name. The natural world has inspired me to find beauty, meaning and power in spoken and written language, and to have the confidence to use this when often words will re-order and reinvent themselves before I have had the chance to speak them. Our existence alongside, and dependence on, our natural environment is inextricably linked with our ability to communicate with it, to understand the beautifully complex language of the land, to care for it, and to express this through creativity.

Some poems are standalone, some have images alongside them. At the back of the collection is a link to an online album of tunes and songs which correspond with many of the poems in the book. Each poem which has its own music has the name of the track with the title. The album is free to listen to, so you can enjoy the holistic experience of this collection, but there is a pay-as-you-feel option if you would like to support my work.

Lastly, why 'As the Flow Cries'? I enjoy playing with spoonerisms and the phrase 'as the crow flies' came to mind. Switching the 'c' and the 'f' suggested a mildly wild, incoherent, yet playful narrative – one which progresses the further one ventures through the collection. Enjoy the ride!

I have felt my mind gracefully ebbing away into the soil. I have witnessed it jetting around in angular fantasies, clinging onto petals, tepals, newness of vocabulary stored generously in underground fungal networks. Mycorrhizae. The freshness, yet depth, of the language of nature is balm to a brain that is parched from a word-overdose, blankets of conversation that leave me drained. Words that leave the lips of humans are riddled with social complexities, they are indeterminable and fly in directions that I am yet to discover. I find solace in the gentleness of nature and the invitation to drink in its conversation without the necessity for correctness in my response, or a response at all. Nature is like music. It is not linear, but has a glorious woven song that is both directional and inert; present yet timeless.

Morning

Song: 'Arise'

Soak: blue sky, green
shoots look up, hopeful.
Hope, in its fullness,
watching brush-marks of cloud
glaze sky in
morning hush.

Look up: see now
with clear vision
aided by the
gentle,
expectant
morning.

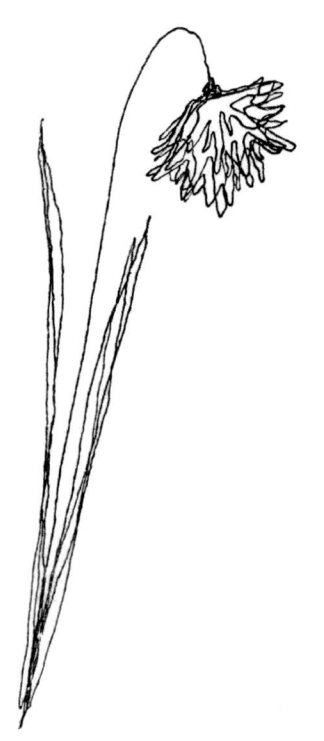

Wet day

Wind swept heather over moor,
brushed breath from bog-sodden walker
sheltered in bothy.

Cloud, full, released itself.
Siling rain dropped;
weighted magnet of wet attracted to walker, drooped,
waited a while before relieving itself.
Cloud or walker?
Water flowing from both,
abundantly.

Slow walk

Tune: 'Wandering Music'

Autumn dusk.
Shrunken fingers grip sleeve,
frost encases skin
creeping, shallow air kisses mist -
freezing thought and time as foot treads
earth, bare and muted.

Piercing blackbird, final call
as light fades to ink,
consuming yet content.

I know

I know, I know.

This Earth-furnace
sheds a layer a year,
sweats a little.

No sweat.

I know, I know.

Meadow sits, naked,
stripped of tree
stripped of skin.
Crisis?

Not yet.

But
    I know
        capercaillie, oystercatcher, merlin,
        carbon-capturing bog.
    Knowledge breeds compassion,
        captures attention,

                              cultivates action?

There is a loss, too   Tune: 'Found Sound'

I listen to blackbird, robin, bluetit.
Scratch of gravel.
Strimmer. Plane.
                    Silence.
I listen to the loss
of sound,
too.

Along the gravel path
there is a loss of sound.
A loss of redwing, bullfinch, nuthatch.

They say silence is golden but
the silence of goldfinch
on
        this
              walk
                      is, should
                              be
                                  a

siren.

Language is action

They spill out,
torrent overflowing
from a landscape
hewn by boredom.

Boredom mutes word and leaf,
need for speed smothers eloquence,
stifles imagination.

Without curiosity,
without an open landscape,
our minds will dim –
are dimming –
as the forest around us
stands,
thinning.

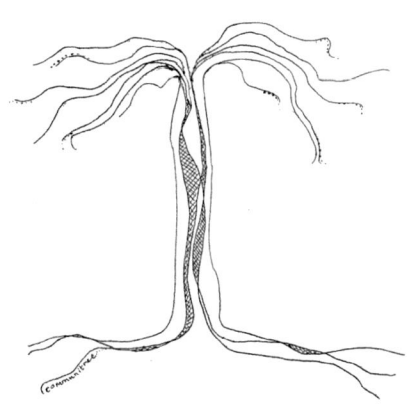

To live time

is to bend to forest floor.
Listen to wing vibration in pollinated bud.
Stroke the gentle green of moss –
Northern fir moss, Huperzia selago –
to allow time for identification,
to stop mid-track (in earth and thought),
to allow time to dwell, to smell, to write.
To hear the daylight call of barn owl and stand in awe.
Ponder the checkerboard surface of freshly-felled stump. Take time
to question. Allow joy to sweep you up in the tide of an answer.

Embrace the parenthesis of thought.

Get a little lost. Only then will you encounter beetle colony, hear the rustle of shell on leaf. Be a guest.
Take the slow route, scimaunder along the path,
you may touch
the edge
of
life.

Convenience

Plastic encases spoon,
each a wrap of their own.
'Each to their own,' they say
when dilemmas run riot:
can Earth survive
on a plastic diet?

Our fast-paced taste
will suffocate,
'Danger of suffocation' not only from bag
but for our future.

Seal lies ensnared in plastic
as we take a quaff of convenience.

Climate crisis

Fixated on clockface,
slowness of time her obsession,
small, wild child counts seconds.
Seconds count
when Earth is under oppression.
Leaders lead us through time,
guiding and assuring of its stability.
Time is an avalanche,
a melting ice cap bulldozing through
man-made minutes. Politicians claim we're at our limits
whilst living time inside
wild child's clockface:
soothingly slow?

Enamel

Enamel,
Western and well-placed.
Cared for,
perfection an obsession.

Enamel,
worn through conflict.
Worn and forgotten,
worn with pride.

Enamel,
encasing Earth.
Fractured and depleting
through tossed question:
'What's it worth?'

When the tents burn   Tune: 'Their Wild'

do we still live our small-scale existence?
Little moments celebrated, cherished,
'Embrace and nourish the Self' is our mantra,
a battle cry in the war waged on blandness, normality,
community.

When the battle cries
do we laugh our discomfort away?
Firing righteousness with Important Topics within our Western frame,
we become eco-warriors overnight
whilst small boy lies motionless in a nest of molten canvas.

When the headlines inundate and overwhelm,
will we be disturbed from our feel-good, do-good stupor?

It is well to pursue health,
search for wildness,
be the naturalist –
but our wild is their wild,
the same trees lie motionless in felled forest
as in Rafah camp under fire.

Field to for -

Song: 'I Lie Down'

- got how to live.
We once sewed and gathered
and found life in natural form,
uncoated.
Found 'being' when it wasn't novel,
was not 'en vogue'.
'Being' was natural, was found
on the land.
We found each other.

Now our business is busyness and
'doing,' a pearl necklace,
a status symbol cutting the circulation
whilst we circulate our lives, our success
over devices
to invisible consumers.
We consume life at a pace that escapes us
whilst we mourn our loss of time
and medicate our migraines.

We are wild as the land we tear apart
and from which we pick daisies.
Let us braid chains that
connect us to our home and
to the vitality of other
breath.

What is your name?   *Song: 'What is Your Name?'*

I want to know
the name
of the yellow stretch of greeting
waving up urban brick wall.

What is your name, little flower?
What makes you stand tall?

There is poetry in your posture,
melody in your gaze.
I want to hold the gaze
of the eyes
you see me through.

Why name the newest star
when we cannot name you?

'...We should receive from every flower, not merely a beautiful image to which the label 'flower' has been affixed, but the full impact of its unimaginable beauty and wonder, the direct sensation of life having communion with life.' [1]

---

[1] Underhill, Evelyn. 1914. *Practical Mysticism*. M. Dent.

River

Song: 'River'

Shapeless is the water that ties
fragile bonds
of common and meadow;
yet,
you sculpt the earth
with your purposeful wander.

River, so bold in your artistry,
shapeless body shaping land
to the sea.

Wind

Tune: 'Wind'

She swings:
moody repetition of
breath through
shafts of time.
Signature cry
whittles window.

Pain is her gift,
but she is change-bringer,
sunlight sings in her wake
as she swings past,
says goodbye.

Wren

Tune: 'Wren'

Rendered helpless by Winter,
Wren did fly less, survive less.
Cold clipped wings into
sculptures of ice –
froze her into the season.

Absence unnoted

until by chance, by cheek,
tail catches eye,
her eye catches mine
through soup-steamed window,
she poses – a wriggling, pulsing sculpture
shattering her shell of frost.

Curlew

Tune: 'Curlew'

Coddiwompler, you yodel on
your erratic flight
shearing through riptides of wind,
encircling,
enraptured
by your directionless mission.

Turtle dove

Tune: 'Turtle Dove'

Echo of call
reflects splinter of light,
a shaft of life in
canopy, encircled in mist.
She calls:
curl of overtone splits air,
wing sculpts its breath.
Her breath is steady
in its music.
Listen.

Blackbird

Tune: 'Blackbird'

You are the overture that sets the sunrise.
Conductor of light,
your morning call carries me
from Now to Then;
you have sung my day, my life.

Yet your morning call
is a mourning call,
a lament for the songs we do not hear,
will not hear
until we lose control
with grace,
joining your lament,
singing with you until the dusk,
calling for the diminishing chorus
to sing in the dawn.

Wake the night

Wake the night.
Night holds creation
    of new, of
        freedom
            holds imagination.
Wake of thought, awake in night
    like an owl, let us refashion
        this wake of birds.
To be a bird is not
    to surrender
      self
          to
              world.
Be like an owl.
Awake the night,
        full,
            bright.

Wild

Song: 'Wild'

She is a wild one,
figure of mind
dancing among the entanglement of words,
overcooked.
She figures they know
the language of order,
of words that speak
with direction, with ease.

But she knows the music,
Disorder of word respun through melody.
In melody, her meaning, speaking, receiving.

The language of many
may not be the melody of few.
Come, listen, she sings.
They did,
and so
      have
            you.

Flow

Why can't I walk into the darkness without turning to the lamp, fear of hooded stranger,
I would rather tramp – feet searching,
knowing
the path through the wilderness rather than the tiptoe of

[pause for breath]

slippered feet across polished floorboards – worried
that hiding in the insular, island-oriented darkness is another ready to pounce
rather than the lynx, the boar that should roam – every ounce
of me wants to beat

[pause
      for breath]

more quickly,
to be wild.

Thaw

Melting my life
like sun
on frost,
glistening.

marker of liminality,
bringer of Spring,
season-shifter,
warmth-awaiting,
snow-defying,
drop of hope.

Heaven on Earth

Heaven is nesting among the feathered pillows
with the early evening sun resting,
gently,
in their invitation.
A fine autumn evening
with the cool breeze
caressing cheek, and all the other
idioms and clichés we use
in moments of perfection.
She inhabits grey plains,
occupied territories,
desolate canopies.
Inhabiting, inviting,
a hope-signature over land
that could not conceive
her embrace.

Wonder

Tune: 'Tree Conversations'

I wonder what it is
to wander
lonely as a pine without wood.
Lost, hairless spine, woody comfort
in upright strength.
I wonder whether pine would
topple, would stumble
without wood;
whether wood holds hairless spine,
magnet in other pine, better
together.

        Fine?

Clarity

Clinging to clarity
like a rock –
steady enough to
fly on netted wings,
I soar.
I saw perspective slip down to me
like an eel
dropped from a puffin's beak.

As unlikely as this
was the clarity to which
I clung.

Good things come to those who   Tune: 'Stray'

wander along the Stray
mind astray
a stray thought meanders
along a path the foot treads

Wait
Halt the doing
Feel the Now as you are
gently
      enveloped
           in being

It is a human thing
Landscape holds power
to free the forceful tide of Should
      the consuming Should

Should do
      better to be

You can

hold your head low.
The sky may not allow for
time, for feeling, lament, breathing.
Why hold your head high when
a soil-bound gaze lets blood flow.
Ally with gravity, lie in the grass.
The mountain need not be scaled today.

Perspective

Tune: 'Darkening and Moss'

Crouch, low.
Smell musky vitality of soil,
life enabler.

Ground perspective.

See life at lower level,
let blood settle to heel.

Rise up from soil,
release inner mole.

Scrape away old earth
and emerge, blinking,
as the crow flies overhead
thinking,
*What it would be
to live life low!*

Beginning

Song: 'Beginning'

As the soil finds healing,
water seeping, sun-seeking,
shoots of beauty may grow
from once-parched land.

As chaos of twigs strewn
over dappled glade
find meaning and purpose
in nest of jay,
so too our chaos and brokenness
pulse on.

There is no need
to quantify, to fully realise –
just be.
Let the light find you
and ignite this
nest
of
chaos.

May it take flight.

*let the soil
of this bud rest
in a little chaos.*

ENDING THOUGHTS

It is natural to feel connected. We are made for, in, with the Wild; yet, nature would rather not be saved. She needs our attention, our love - not our proposals, our policies. Nature has lived, and still lives without us, too. The heather does not cease to be purple under the blackout night.

Thank you for journeying with me.

THE ALBUM

You can find my accompanying album to this collection through the Bandcamp link here: https://laurasutcliffe.bandcamp.com/album/as-the-flow-cries

The creation and production of this album is natural and raw, drawing on the sound of the 'now' as if you were in the room, avoiding the glossiness of studio production. It is a daringly unedited approach to musicking and recording, capturing the realness and vulnerability of both the focussed and the abstract – human, animal, and environmental sounds.

THE AUTHOR

Laura is a musician, writer and artist based in Yorkshire. She enjoys sharing her work through informal and participatory performances, particularly welcoming those who appreciate a relaxed and unimposing environment.

She also works as a community musician, bringing together unlikely people in unlikely spaces, making unlikely (but mostly lovely) sounds, pictures, songs, stories, and movement.

Outside work (though often providing the inspiration for it), Laura spends most of her time meandering through the countryside, frequenting bookshops, baking gluten-free bread, creating tahini-based sauces, and fermenting rather a lot of cabbage.

You can find Laura on Instagram, @musicpoet_laura.